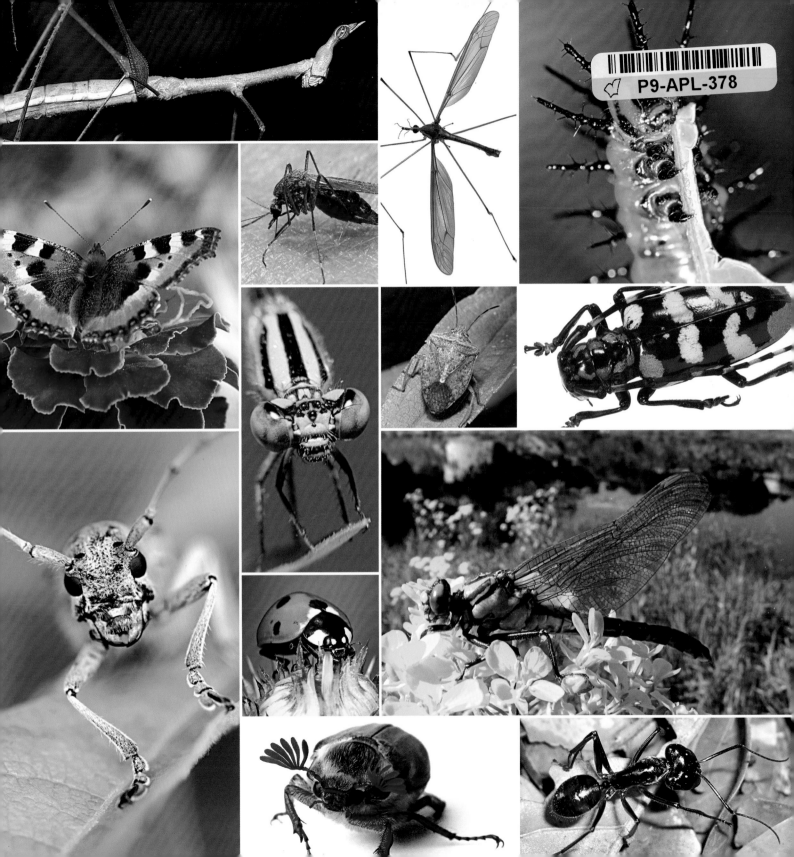

"LOBSTER LEARNERS" SERIES

DON'T SQUASH THAT BUG!

The Curious Kid's Guide to Insects

written by

Natalie Rompella

Lobster Press ™

To my students – past, present, and future.
– Natalie Rompella

Don't Squash That Bug! The Curious Kid's Guide to Insects
Text © 2007 Natalie Rompella

Published by Lobster Press™
1620 Sherbrooke Street West, Suites C & D
Montréal, Québec   H3H 1C9
Tel. (514) 904-1100 • Fax (514) 904-1101 • www.lobsterpress.com

Publisher: Alison Fripp
Editors: Alison Fripp & Meghan Nolan
Editorial Assistants: Katie Scott & Olga Zoumboulis
Graphic Design & Production: Tammy Desnoyers
Production Assistant: Luanna Venditti

Content evaluated by Zack Lemann, Staff Entomologist with Audubon Nature Institute,
and Steve Sullivan, curator at the Chicago Academy of Sciences and Notebaert Nature Museum.

Library and Archives Canada Cataloguing in Publication

Rompella, Natalie, 1974-
        Don't squash that bug!: the curious kid's guide to insects / Natalie Rompella ; Margo Burian, illustrator.

(Lobster learners series)
ISBN-13: 978-1-897073-50-6 (bound)
ISBN-10: 1-897073-50-X (bound)

        1. Insects--Juvenile literature. I. Burian, Margo II. Title. III. Series.

QL467.2.R6513 2007   j595.7   C2006-905146-1

Front cover (from top, moving down): dragonfly, ladybug

Title page (from top, moving down): praying mantid, ladybug, dragonfly

Back cover (from top right corner, moving clockwise): lightning bug (also called a firefly), lime butterflies, hornet, flower beetle, praying mantid, bee pollinating a flower, ladybug

Front and back endsheets: Use the categories in the book to identify each one of these creatures.
Check your answers at: www.lobsterpress.com

Printed and bound in Canada.

Insects. Buzzing, flying, chirping, crawling, swimming. Some even glow or foam. In this book you will learn about many different insects and their special characteristics.

But first, how do you know if a creature is an insect? It's an insect if it has six legs. Insects also have three body parts: a head, a middle part called a 🦋 *thorax*, and a back section called an 🦋 *abdomen*. Each insect has a hard layer on the outside of its body. This is its 🦋 *exoskeleton*, which means "outside skeleton."

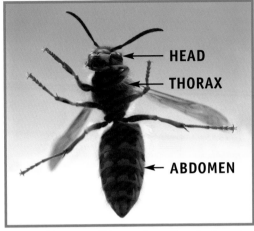
▲ *Like this wasp, all insects have three body parts.*

▲ *Ants care for their eggs and protect them from predators.*

Nearly all insects start out as eggs, but not all insects change to adults in the same way. Some may change from an egg to a 🦋 *nymph*, which looks like a smaller version of the adult insect. Other insects have what's called a 🦋 *larval* stage. At this stage, they look very different from the adult insect they will become (see **Butterflies and Moths**).

▲ *Praying mantid nymphs look like the adult praying mantids without wings.*

▲ *Caterpillars are butterfly or moth larvae.*

LET'S GET STARTED!

Are you ready to find out more about insects? Along the way, you'll also come across the following:

ORDER:

Just as you might help sort the laundry by characteristics such as color, scientists organize insects by placing them into categories. "Order" is a category in which insects with similar features are grouped together. On the top of each page, you will find the name scientists use for each insect order.

Don't Squash That Bug!

Discover how each type of insect is important to humans, other animals, and plants.

Country Cousin

Insects live all over the world. Find out about some that are related to the ones in your own backyard.

Where Are They?

Find out where to look for different insects!

WORD LIST

As you read, you'll also come across the words below.
(Words marked with a 🦋 throughout the book are explained on this page.)

abdomen (AB duh muhn) the last section of an insect's body

antennae (an TEHN ee) a pair of organs on an insect's head used for smelling or feeling

camouflage (KAM uh flahzh) to blend in with a background

carnivore (KAHR nuh vawr) a meat eater

chrysalis (KRIHS uh lihs) the pupa stage of a butterfly; it forms when a caterpillar molts for the last time

cocoon (kuh KOON) what a caterpillar that will become a moth spins out of silk and other material, such as a leaves, to cover itself while it changes into an adult

decompose (DEE kuhm POHZ) to rot

entomologist (EHN tuh MOL uh jihst) a person who studies insects

exoskeleton (EHK soh SKEHL uh tuhn) hard, outer covering of an insect

herbivore (HUR buh vawr) a plant eater

insectivore (ihn SEHK tuh vawr) an insect eater

larva (LAHR vuh) the early stage of most insects; it's usually "wormy" looking like a caterpillar or a maggot, and it will look completely different when it becomes an adult

larvae (LAHR vee) more than one larva

metamorphosis (MEHT uh MAWR fuh sihs) a change in form

mimicry (MIHM ihk ree) when an insect looks like something it is not, such as another insect or a part of a plant, in order to gain protection from predators

molt (mohlt) to shed the exoskeleton

nectar (NEHK tuhr) a sugary liquid produced by flowers that is an important food for many insects

nymph (nihmf) the early stage of many insects; a nymph looks like a small adult insect

omnivore (AHM nuh vawr) a creature that eats both plants and animals

pest (pehst) an organism that causes injury or harm to another living thing

pollen (PAHL uhn) a powdery substance found in most flowers

pollination (PAHL uh NAY shuhn) the process of carrying pollen from one flower to another; pollination helps flowers and fruit to grow

predator (PREHD uh tuhr) an animal that hunts another animal for food

prey (pray) an animal that is hunted by another animal for food

proboscis (proh BAHS ihs) the straw-like mouthpart found on some insects, such as a butterflies

proleg (PROH lehg) a back "leg" on a caterpillar that helps it grip or hold on to surfaces

pupa (PYOO puh) the stage between a larva and adult that usually has a protective covering, such as a chrysalis or cocoon

scavenger (SKAV uhn juhr) a creature that eats decaying material

thorax (THAWR aks) the middle section of an insect's body

True Bugs

Scentless plant bugs may join you indoors when the weather cools down. They are harmless.

Don't Squash That Bug!

Although some true bugs are *pests*, others eat the pests. Wheel bugs are often helpful because they eat pest bugs.

Leaf-footed bugs can have unusual back legs that look like leaves. ▼

▲ A bug cleans its beak-like mouth by running it through its front legs.

ORDER: Hemiptera (hih MIHP tuhr uh),

which means "half wings." The first half of the front wings is thicker than the rest of the wings.

▲ *A stink bug lets off an odor to scare away enemies.*

Did you know that bugs are a type of insect? Often we call all insects "bugs," even though many of them are not part of this order. True bugs include stink bugs, water striders, and squash bugs. They have a beak-like mouthpart. Some eat plants and some eat other insects. Giant water bugs can eat frogs and fish!

Water striders are also called "pond skaters," ▲
since they skate on the surface of the water.

◀ *A wheel bug, a kind of assassin bug, preys on a caterpillar.*

Where Are They?

Most true bugs live on land, but some live in the water, such as water striders.

Where Are They?

A buzzing noise in the trees comes from cicadas. These insects lay eggs in branches. When the 🦋 **nymphs** hatch, they fall to the ground where they can suck on the plant's roots. The nymphs live in the soil until they are ready to become adults. Then they find a vertical surface, such as tree bark or a fence, to help them 🦋 **molt**, and finally they fly away. In the fall, look for empty cicada shells near trees.

Cicadas, Treehoppers, Aphids, and More

Some species of cicadas can take up to seventeen years before they become adults.

◄ *Lanternflies are among the more highly patterned and colorful-winged homopterans.*

Aphids, like this colony, feed on plant juices. ▼

ORDER: Homoptera (hoh MOP tuhr uh),

which means "same wings."

Can you believe that an insect as small as a drop of water can be a big problem for a farmer? Aphids, cicadas, treehoppers, scale insects, and white-flies, all part of the Homoptera order, are insects that cause lots of trouble. They are 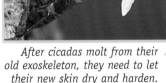 *herbivores*, or plant eaters, and because many of them can multiply so fast and eat so much, they can destroy a farmer's crop quickly.

Treehoppers have a large pronotum, which is a section of their thorax.

After cicadas molt from their old exoskeleton, they need to let their new skin dry and harden.

◀ *Spittlebug nymphs hide in a layer of bubbles.*

Leafhoppers can be as short as a sesame seed or as long as a gummy bear. ▼

Don't Squash That Bug!

Aphids are *pests* to crops and plants, but they are helpful to other insects. Aphids produce a substance called honeydew, which is used by ants for food. The bees can use it to make honey, but it doesn't have much flavor.

Flies

Country Cousin

Different kinds of flies can be found around the world. One species of fungus gnat lives in caves in New Zealand. Its 🦋 *larvae* glow in the dark! You can find fungus gnats in your own home. They are the little black flies that are found near over-watered house-plants.

Flies have many facets to their eyes. In many kinds of flies, it is easy to tell the males from the females ▼ because male flies have larger eyes.

Crane flies don't eat mosquitoes or bite humans, as many people think. ▲

ORDER: Diptera (DIHP tuhr uh),

which means "two wings."

What can be more annoying than a fly buzzing around your house? Itchy mosquito bites! Both of these insects, along with fruit flies and gnats, belong to the Diptera order. Like helicopters, flies can hover and move backward. They can even land upside down!

House flies sometimes move into houses when the weather is cold.

Only female mosquitoes bite. When they do, they inject their saliva under your skin, which makes you itch.

Flies, like almost all insects, have compound eyes. If you look closely, you will see that the eyes have many sides, like a soccer ball. This helps them see movement quickly.

◀ *Flies help to pollinate flowers, even ones that are not sweetly scented.*

Don't Squash That Bug!

Flies are helpful to nature. Some flies move ❁ **pollen** from one flower to another, which creates fruit and seeds. This is called ❁ **pollination**. Some of the flowers that flies pollinate smell like rotting meat. Not too many other insects are attracted to that smell! Flies also help ❁ **decompose**, or break down, dead plants and animals.

Beetles

Country Cousin

The Goliath beetle is as long as a soda can! It is found mostly in the African rainforests.

Beetles have transparent wings protected beneath their hard outer wings.

Elderberry longhorn beetle larvae live in elderberry bushes. Some species are threatened because the bushes are being cut down.

▲ Dung beetles are in the scarab beetle family.

ORDER: Coleoptera (KOH lee AHP tuh ruh),

which means "sheath wings." A sheath is a covering. The hard wings that beetles have are like a coat of armor.

Beetles are many different colors and sizes. They live on land, in the air, and in the water. Some beetles in your backyard are ladybugs (on low plants), longhorn beetles (on trees), and ground beetles (under rocks). You might also see beetle *larvae*, which include grubs and mealworms. Did you know that there are more beetles than any other type of insect? Most beetles are *herbivores*. This means they eat only plants. Nearly all beetles have a set of hard outer wings for protection and thin wings underneath for flying.

There are more than 350,000 kinds of beetles. A relative of this flower beetle is the size of a pencil eraser.

▲ *Stag beetles use their jaws to fight predators.*

Beetles go through complete metamorphosis. The larvae look totally different from the adults.

◀ *The many species of ladybugs have different numbers and colors of spots.*

Don't Squash That Bug!

Some beetles are helpful. Farmers buy ladybugs to eat the aphids on their crops. Aphids are *pests* to plants because they suck the juice out of their leaves. A ladybug can eat 5,000 aphids in its lifetime! (See **Cicadas, Treehoppers, Aphids, and More** to learn about aphids.)

Termites

Country Cousin

Imagine a termite mound as tall as four elephants! That is how tall some termite mounds are in Australia and Africa.

Termite mounds are made from mud and a cement-like liquid the termites produce. ▼

ORDER: Isoptera (eye SAHP tuhr uh),

which means "equal wings."

How would you like to be king or queen? Termites live in mounds or underground mazes and have a king and queen, soldier termites, and worker termites. The queen can live up to 30 years! The soldiers defend the mound. The workers' job is to build the mound and find food for other termites.

A queen termite can lay tens of thousands of eggs in a day. Her abdomen, which holds the eggs, is large, making it difficult for her to move around.

Where Are They?

Look for termites in dead and rotting wood, since that is what they like to eat. We have insects, such as termites, to thank for getting rid of this material.

◀ *Many winged termites will find a mate, lose their wings, and then start their own colony.*

Some species of termites can cause ▲ damage to houses and buildings because they eat wood, but in the wild, they are valuable as decomposers.

Country Cousin

One of the largest ant colonies ever found was in Australia. It was 62 miles long. That's almost the width of New Hampshire!

Bees, Wasps, and Ants

▲ Ants are eaten in some countries, some even coated in chocolate.

◀ Ants care for their young. Notice the queen red ant in the circle.

▲ Some flowers have an ultraviolet color that bees can see but people can't. The flowers glow like targets to direct the bees to the nectar source.

Honeybees make honey from flower ▶ nectar and a chemical in their bodies.

ORDER: Hymenoptera (HY muh NAHP tuhr uh),

which means "membraned wings." A membrane is a thin, flimsy layer.

Bees, wasps, and ants are part of the same order because they all have a narrow "waist" where their 🦋 **thorax** and **abdomen** connect and because their front wings are larger than their back wings. Did you know that some ants have wings and some wasps do not? Worker ants never have wings. Neither do some female wasps. Queen and male ants have wings at first but then lose them.

Bees' wings move about 200 times a second.

▼ *Just like bees, wasps pollinate flowers.*

Many bees, wasps, and ants have stingers, so be careful! When some bees sting, their stinger (and important organs) stay behind, which causes them to die.

▲ *Paper wasps make nests out of chewed-up wood mixed with saliva.*

Some bees and wasps and all ants live in colonies. Ant colonies have sections like rooms. They have eating rooms, rooms to care for the eggs, and rooms for garbage.

Don't Squash That Bug!

We get fruit from flowers that have been 🦋 **pollinated** by such insects as bees. Honeybees also give us honey by mixing 🦋 **nectar**, the liquid inside a flower, with a special chemical inside their stomachs. They then put the mixture into honeycombs, and beekeepers take it out for us to use. To make one jar of honey, it may take bees more than a million trips from flowers to the honeycomb.

Stick and Leaf Insects

Country Cousin

Walking sticks usually live where it's warm. In southeast Asia, there is a stick insect 14 inches long. That's longer than a ruler!

Most stick insects have a weak joint in their legs that allows them to lose a leg in order to escape from predators.

▼ Leaf insects mimic leaves.

▲ Peruvian fire stick insects are brightly colored to warn predators to stay away.

ORDER: Phasmatodea (FAZ muh TOH dee uh),

which means "looks like a ghost." They can be hard to see since they camouflage themselves so well.

◀ *Stick insects are herbivores.*

Have you ever played freeze tag? Stick and leaf insects play their own version of it all the time. When they are standing still, they look just like sticks or leaves. This is called ✖ *camouflage*, and it helps them to stay hidden from predators.

Giant prickly stick insects have sharp spines that keep predators away. ▼

Where Are They?

Walking sticks, a kind of stick insect, can be found in and near trees, where they look just like twigs. The next time you see a twig, look closer – it could be an insect!

Butterflies and Moths

Country Cousin

In many countries, moth caterpillars, often called silkworms, are valued for their silk. When the caterpillars spin their cocoons, the silk is collected and used to make fabric.

Butterflies have compound eyes and a straw-like "tongue" called a proboscis.

A caterpillar holds on to a twig with its six small true legs as well as with the large prolegs on the back of its body. ▼

▲ *To make a silk shirt, it can take 1,000 silkworm cocoons!*

When a butterfly emerges from its chrysalis, its wings must dry and harden before it can fly away.

ORDER: Lepidoptera (LEHP uh DAHP tuhr uh),

which means "scaled wings."

Common buckeye butterflies have spots on their wings that look like large eyes to predators.

Caterpillars are the 🦋 *larva* stage of butterflies and moths. The last sets of their legs have little suction cups. These are called 🦋 *prolegs*, which are used to hold on to surfaces.

▲ Butterflies and moths, such as this luna moth, need to pump fluid from their abdomen into their wings.

What's the difference between moths and butterflies? Moths are usually awake at night while butterflies are awake during the day. Another difference is the way in which they become adults. A moth caterpillar usually covers itself with silk – this is called a 🦋 *cocoon*. A butterfly caterpillar forms a 🦋 *chrysalis*, which is a special name for its 🦋 *pupa*.

Butterflies and moths have very fragile wings made up of scales, kind of like fish scales. If you touch these insects, be very careful because you could accidentally break their wings.

◀ *Main photo on opposite page: Rice paper butterflies have white wings that look like rice paper.*

Where Are They?

If you find chewed leaves, you might find a newly hatched, hungry caterpillar nearby. Unlike caterpillars, butterflies only drink. If you watch a butterfly carefully, you will see it unroll its 🦋 *proboscis*, a long, straw-like tongue, to drink nectar from a flower. As butterflies reach inside flowers for nectar, pollen sticks to them. The pollen then helps the next flower that they land on produce fruit and seeds.

Dragonflies

Insect wings are connected to the thorax, as you can see in this close-up picture.

Like this darner dragonfly, all winged insects, except those in the fly order, have four wings. ▲

Where Are They?

Because dragonflies lay their eggs in the water, look for them in their ✖ *nymph* stage there. When they are adults, you will still see them flying near water.

▲ Dragonflies emerge from their last molt with wings.

ORDER: Odonata (oh duh NAH tuh),

which means "toothed ones." They have strong mandibles, or jaws, they use to eat other insects, their prey. Dragonflies mean no harm to humans and don't bite us.

Sometimes male and female insects of the same species look different. Only male common whitetails have white abdomens.

Millions of years ago, some dragonflies had wings that were about 27 inches from tip to tip. Damselflies belong in the same group as dragonflies. They are smaller and usually rest with their wings together. True dragonflies rest with their wings straight out.

Dragonfly nymphs can live in the water from three months to a few years before they emerge to become adults.

Dragonflies are fantastic acrobats: they can hover, fly sideways, and even fly backwards.

◀ Dragonflies and damselflies usually have transparent wings.

Don't Squash That Bug!

Dragonflies are **predators**, which means they attack and eat other creatures. While they are in their nymph stage, they eat water creatures. As adults, they feast on many insects, including **pests**, such as mosquitoes, gnats, and flies.

Grasshoppers and Crickets

Country Cousin

Cave crickets' 🦋 **an-tennae** are very long so they can smell and feel around their whole body in the dark. Cave crickets live in northern Africa and southern Europe, as well as North America.

You can tell this is a male cricket because it has two long organs, called cerci, at the end of its abdomen.

Grasshoppers use their mandibles to chew leaves. ▼

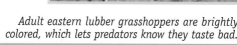

Adult eastern lubber grasshoppers are brightly colored, which lets predators know they taste bad. ▼

▲ Most crickets and grasshoppers have wings that cover their abdomens when they are done growing. This grasshopper is still a nymph.

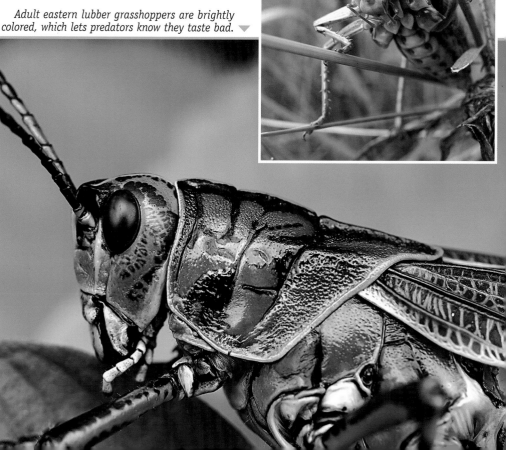

ORDER: Orthoptera (awr THAHP tuhr uh),

which means "straight wings."

Grasshoppers' back legs have ▲
muscles that help them to jump.

Did you know that grasshoppers can jump about 20 times their body length? This would be like a child moving from one end of a basket-ball court to the other in one jump. Grasshoppers have very strong back legs that help them jump away from 🦋 **predators**. They also use 🦋 **camou-flage** to blend in with trees and fields. Katydids, which are related to grasshoppers and crickets, have wings that look like leaves. This makes them hard to see in forests and fields. Because most male crickets, grasshoppers, and katydids make noise, follow the sounds to find them.

Female crickets bury their eggs by sticking their ovipositor into the ground.

▲ *Katydids mimic leaves. Most are green, but there are brown ones as well.*

Katydids sing mostly at night.

Don't Squash That Bug!

You can figure out the tempera-ture by listening to certain crickets. Count the number of chirps in 13 seconds. Then add 40 to that number. It will give you the temperature in Fahrenheit.

Cockroaches

Hissing cockroaches can be three inches long. They do not bite.

Country Cousin

The hissing cockroach from Madagascar makes a noise by pushing air out of its breathing holes, which are called spiracles. Some people actually keep these as pets!

ORDER: Blattodea (blat toh DEE uh)

"Blatta" is the Latin word for "cockroach."

Cockroaches are very fast runners. They escape from 🦋 *predators* by being quick and by fitting into small spaces. There are different species of cockroaches. German cockroaches are small and brown. The American cockroach is larger. Cockroaches are 🦋 *omnivores*, which means they eat plants and animals. They will even eat the glue on the backs of postage stamps.

▲ *American cockroaches live where there may be food scraps, such as in restaurants and kitchens.*

▲ *Cockroaches usually hide during the day and come out at night.*

◀ *Cockroach nymphs, such as these giant cave cockroaches, do not have wings.*

Don't Squash That Bug!

Most people do not like cockroaches, but they are 🦋 *scavengers*, which means they eat dead plants and animals. They are also some of the oldest insects still around – they lived before dinosaurs!

Praying Mantids

Country Cousin

A praying mantid with stripes? A mantid that looks like a dead leaf? Praying mantids all around the world have coloring and wing shapes that help them blend in with their surroundings. In north Africa and southern Europe, the Devil's Flower Mantis lives in flowers, where being striped might help it *camouflage* itself.

Some praying mantids have stripes to camouflage themselves in grass, just as zebras do. This one even has bumpy eyes that look like blades of grass. ▶

▼ *Mantids sometimes wait near flowers for insects to come close enough for them to eat.*

ORDER: Mantodea (Man toh DEE uh),

which means "looks like a fortune teller." It is thought that praying mantids stand in a position similar to that of someone who predicts the future.

Praying mantids (or praying mantises) can attack hummingbirds, frogs, small lizards, small rodents, and most insects. They are *insectivores* and *carnivores*, meaning they eat other insects and animals. They usually eat creatures that are still alive. They watch their *prey* and then snatch it quickly before it has time to escape.

Using their strong and sharp front legs, praying mantids grip their prey.

Praying mantids have very good eyesight for spotting their prey. ▼

Praying mantids can ▲ catch their prey as fast as you can blink.

◀ The Chinese mantid was brought to America to help control pest insects.

Insects All Around

Magnifying glasses are lenses that help ▲ to make small objects appear larger.

Next time you go outside, bring a magnifying glass with you so that you can look closer at the insects all around.

- Look near flowers for flies and butterflies, but watch out for bees and wasps.

Many moths use the moon to guide them through the night sky.

- Look under stones, leaves, and dead wood for ground beetles, termites, cockroaches, and ants.

- Look in the air for butterflies, moths, beetles, bugs, dragonflies, flies, bees, and wasps.

- Look in the grass for crickets, ants, praying mantids, bugs, beetles, and grasshoppers.

◀ Ants live on every continent but Antarctica.

- Look in the trees for cicadas, caterpillars, beetles, bugs, stick insects, katydids, and ants.

- Look in the water for dragonfly nymphs, beetles, and bugs.

▲ We need insects like bees to pollinate flowers so that fruit can grow.

▲ There are more beetles than any other species of insect.

Cicadas are sometimes easier to hear than see.

Try going outside at different times of the day to see different insects. If you go out at night, you might want to look near a light or bring one out with you as insects are attracted to light. Certain colors attract insects, too. Bright colors and pinks and reds may attract butterflies. You may want to avoid blues and yellows, since these colors attract bees.

You might have to look carefully to see insects, like this praying mantid, since they use camouflage so well.

You might decide to collect an insect in a jar with holes in it so that you can take a closer look. If you do this, be careful, and be sure to let the insect go where you found it.

You can now be considered a junior *entomologist*, a person who studies insects. This means that you have a very important job – to share with others how special insects are, to let them know where to find them, and to say, "Don't squash that bug!"

Handle only insects that you know will not bite or sting. Some may be too delicate, but others can be fun to hold.

◄ *Don't forget to look for insects like damselflies near ponds.*

▲ *Unlike some insects, spiders do not have two compound eyes. Instead, they have many simple eyes.*

There are many other cool creatures that are not insects. Spiders, for example, belong to a different class. They have eight legs and two body parts: a cephalothorax (SEHF uh loh THOHR aks), which is the head and ✖ **thorax** together, and an ✖ **abdomen**. All have fangs and usually eight eyes.

Another creature that is not an insect is the centipede. Centipedes usually have eighteen segments, or parts, most with legs. They look for food at night and use a poison to kill their prey.

Another creature you may see outside belongs to the order Isopoda (eye suh POH duh). It includes sow bugs and roly-polys. Sometimes roly-polys are called pill bugs. If roly-polys are scared, they will curl up into a ball.

Unlike pill bugs, sow bugs do not curl up into a tight ball. ▲

If you look under rocks and logs, you may be able to find pill bugs. ▼

▲ *Spider silk is stronger than steel of the same size.*